D1528069

VIRTUE
AND VICE

VIRTUE
AND VICE

A DICTIONARY OF
THE GOOD LIFE

C. S. LEWIS

Edited by Patricia S. Klein

 HarperSanFrancisco
A Division of HarperCollinsPublishers

The excerpts from *Virtue and Vice* previously appeared in
other C. S. Lewis books. For a complete list of sources, see
the index of sources quoted and permissions on page 102.

VIRTUE AND VICE: *A Dictionary of the Good Life.*
Copyright © 2005 by C. S. Lewis Pte. Ltd. Edited by
Patricia S. Klein. All rights reserved. Printed in the United
States of America. No part of this book may be used or re-
produced in any manner whatsoever without written per-
mission except in the case of brief quotations embodied in
critical articles and reviews. For information address
HarperCollins Publishers, Inc., 10 East 53rd Street, New
York, NY 10022.

HarperCollins books may be purchased for educational,
business, or sales promotional use. For information please
write: Special Markets Department, HarperCollins Publishers, Inc., 10 East 53rd Street, New York, NY 10022.

HarperCollins Web site: http://www.harpercollins.com

HarperCollins®, 📖®, and HarperSanFrancisco™
are trademarks of HarperCollins Publishers, Inc.

FIRST EDITION

Library of Congress Cataloging-in-Publication Data is
available on request.

ISBN 0–06–076151–2 (hardcover)

05 06 07 08 09 CW 10 9 8 7 6 5 4 3 2 1

INTRODUCTION

Vice and *virtue.* To the modern ear these words convey meanings twisted by our own culture and behavior. The word *vice* sounds benign, describing fundamentally harmless habits and attitudes, the kinds of things normal people do and feel. The word *virtue,* by contrast, communicates a prudish self-righteousness, the sort of character we're not interested in being around, much less becoming.

Of course, the point of redefining these terms is to neutralize them so we can prove that we're not really so bad after all. If vice is just a few bad acts, the occasional vulgarity, and, yes, okay, a bad temper—but who's perfect?—then I'm better than most folks. And if virtue is an annoying holier-than-thou creature, well, let's just set the record straight by proving that that person's not really so great, certainly not better than we are.

Both *virtue* and *vice* have been gutted, stripped of their power, and left empty of truth. Sadly, eviscerating the words does nothing to alter the conditions the words originally described, and then, more sadly still, we are left with no words to describe powerful and real matters. Without the words, how can we ever hope to learn, to understand, to change?

To C. S. Lewis, these words were not empty, bereft of meaning. *Virtue* and *vice* were precise terms, describing specific and vital aspects of good and evil. And for him, good and evil were the ultimate reality. In Lewis's writing, we see a vitality in the workings of good and evil in our lives. Lewis believed,

"We Christians think man lives for ever. Therefore, what really matters is those little marks or twists on the central, inside part of the soul which are going to turn it, in the long run, into a heavenly or a hellish creature." Virtue and vice are not simply passive indicators of character; it turns out that they are also active predictors of future character.

How does that happen? Well, it seems we are participants in shaping our own character. We get to choose; we decide whether it will be evil or good that forms our selves. But it's never the big decisions that trip us up, is it? It's the little choices—the petty untruth, the hidden pilfering, the secret lewdness, the lick of pride or cruelty or selfishness. Each small indulgence makes the next one easier. And it is the small kindness, the unexpected act of courage or forgiveness or charity or duty—each decision for good or virtue— that makes our next decision for good that much easier. Lewis says it best: "Good and evil both increase at compound interest. That is why the little decisions you and I make every day are of such infinite importance. The smallest good act today is the capture of a strategic point from which, a few months later, you may be able to go on to victories you never dreamed of. An apparently trivial indulgence in lust or anger today is the loss of a ridge or railway line or bridgehead from which the enemy may launch an attack otherwise impossible."

Few writers are better than Lewis at exploring and explaining the nuances of good and evil. Gathered here are pieces of Lewis's most vibrant writing on the fundamental matters of virtue and vice—writing in which he unwraps, unmasks, disarms, engages, and in the end, lays before us truth, vivid and irresistible. What we do with this truth, he no doubt would say, is our choice.

—*Patricia S. Klein*

VIRTUE
AND VICE

AMBITION. Ambition! We must be careful what we mean by it. If it means the desire to get ahead of other people—which is what I think it does mean—then it is bad. If it means simply wanting to do a thing well, then it is good. It isn't wrong for an actor to want to act his part as well as it can possibly be acted, but the wish to have his name in bigger type than the other actors is a bad one.

CHARACTER. There is a difference between doing some particular just or temperate action and being a just or temperate man. Someone who is not a good tennis player may now and then make a good shot. What you

I

mean by a good player is a man whose eye and muscles and nerves have been so trained by making innumerable good shots that they can now be relied on. They have a certain tone or quality which is there even when he is not playing, just as a mathematician's mind has a certain habit and outlook which is there even when he is not doing mathematics. In the same way a man who perseveres in doing just actions gets in the end a certain quality of character. Now it is that quality rather than the particular actions which we mean when we talk of a 'virtue'.

CHARITY. 'Charity' now means simply what used to be called 'alms'—that is, giving to the poor. Originally it had a much wider meaning. (You can see how it got the modern sense. If a man has 'charity', giving to the poor is one of the most obvious things he does, and so people came to talk as if that were the whole of charity. In the same way, 'rhyme' is the most obvious thing about poetry, and so people come to mean by 'poetry' simply rhyme and nothing more.) Charity means 'Love, in the Christian sense'. But love, in the Christian sense, does not mean an emotion. It is a state not of the feelings but of the will; that state of the will which we have naturally about ourselves, and must learn to have about other people. . . .

. . . Christian Love (or Charity) for our neighbours is quite a different thing from liking or affection. We 'like' or are 'fond of' some people, and not of others. It is important to understand that this natural 'liking' is neither a sin nor a virtue, any more than your likes and dislikes in food are a sin or a virtue. It is just a fact. But, of course, what we do about it is either sinful or virtuous.

CHARITY, OR ALMS. Charity—giving to the poor—is an essential part of Christian morality: in the frightening parable of the sheep and the goats it seems to be the point on which everything turns. Some people nowadays say that charity ought to be unnecessary and that instead of giving to the poor we ought to be producing a society in which there were no poor to give to. They may be quite right in saying that we ought to produce this kind of society. But if anyone thinks that, as a consequence, you can stop giving in the meantime, then he has parted company with all Christian morality. I do not believe one can settle how much we ought to give. I am afraid the only safe rule is to give more than we can spare. In other words, if our expenditure on comforts, luxuries, amusements, etc., is up to the standard common among those with the same income as our own, we are probably giving away too little. If our charities do not at all pinch or hamper us, I should say they are too small. There ought to be things we should like to do and cannot do because our charities expenditure excludes them. I am speaking now of 'charities' in the common way. Particular cases of distress among your own relatives, friends, neighbours or employees, which God, as it were, forces upon your notice, may demand much more: even to the crippling and endangering of your own position. For many of us the great obstacle to charity lies not in our luxurious living or desire for more money, but in our fear—fear of insecurity. This must often be recognised as a temptation. Sometimes our pride also hinders our charity; we are tempted to spend more than we ought on the showy forms of generosity (tipping, hospitality) and less than we ought on those who really need our help.

CHASTITY. Chastity is the most unpopular of the Christian virtues. There is no getting away from it; the Christian rule is, 'Either marriage, with complete faithfulness to your partner, or else total abstinence.' Now this is so difficult and so contrary to our instincts, that obviously either Christianity is wrong or our sexual instinct, as it now is, has gone wrong. One or the other. Of course, being a

Christian, I think it is the instinct which has gone wrong.

COUNT THE COST. He warned people to 'count the cost' before becoming Christians. 'Make no mistake,' He says, 'if you let me, I will make you perfect. The moment you put yourself in My hands, that is what you are in for. Nothing less, or other, than that. You have free will, and if you choose, you can push Me away. But if you do not push Me away, understand that I am going to see this job through. Whatever suffering it may cost you in your earthly life, whatever inconceivable purification it may cost you after death, whatever it costs Me, I will never rest, nor let you rest, until you are literally perfect—until my Father can say without reservation that He is well pleased with you, as He said He was well pleased with me. This I can do and will do. But I will not do anything less.'

And yet—this is the other and equally important side of it—this Helper who will, in the long run, be satisfied with nothing less than absolute perfection, will also be delighted with the first feeble, stumbling effort you make tomorrow to do the simplest duty. As a great Christian writer (George MacDonald) pointed out, every father is pleased at the baby's first attempt to walk: no father would be satisfied with anything less than a firm, free, manly walk in a grown-up son. In the same way, he said, 'God is easy to please, but hard to satisfy.'

COURAGE AND COWARDICE.

The demon Screwtape writes: We have made men proud of most vices, but not of cowardice. Whenever we have almost succeeded in doing so, the Enemy permits a war or an earthquake or some other calamity, and at once courage becomes so obviously lovely and important even in human eyes that all our work is undone, and there is still at least one vice of which they feel genuine shame. The danger of inducing cowardice in our patients, therefore, is lest we produce real self-knowledge and self-loathing with consequent repentance and humility. And in fact, in the last war, thousands of humans, by discovering their own cowardice, discovered the whole moral world for the first time. In peace we can make many of them ignore good and evil entirely; in danger, the issue is forced upon them in a guise to which even we cannot blind them. There is here a cruel dilemma before us. If we promoted justice and charity among men, we should be playing directly into the Enemy's hands; but if we guide them to the opposite behaviour, this sooner or later produces (for He permits it to produce) a war or a revolution, and the undisguisable issue of cowardice or courage awakes thousands of men from moral stupor.

This, indeed, is probably one of the Enemy's motives for creating a dangerous world—a world in which moral issues really come to the point. He sees as well as you do that courage is not simply *one* of the virtues, but the form of every virtue at the testing point, which means, at the point of highest reality. A chastity or honesty, or mercy, which yields to danger will be chaste or honest or merciful only on conditions. Pilate was merciful till it became risky.

CRUELTY. Are we not really an increasingly cruel age? Perhaps we are: but I think we have become so in the attempt to reduce all virtues to kindness. For Plato rightly taught that virtue is one. You cannot be kind unless you have all the other virtues. If, being cowardly, conceited and slothful, you have never yet done a fellow creature great mischief, that is only because your neighbour's welfare has not yet happened to conflict with your safety, self-approval, or ease. Every vice leads to cruelty. Even a good emotion, pity, if not controlled by charity and justice, leads through anger to cruelty. Most atrocities are stimulated by accounts of the enemy's atrocities; and pity for the oppressed classes, when separated from the moral law as a whole, leads by a very natural process to the unremitting brutalities of a reign of terror.

DESPAIR. *The demon Screwtape observes:* Despair is a greater sin than any of the sins which provoke it.

DUTY. Every duty is a religious duty, and our obligation to perform every duty is therefore absolute. Thus we may have a duty to rescue a drowning man and, perhaps, if we live on a dangerous coast, to learn lifesaving so as to be ready for any drowning man when he turns up. It may be our duty to lose our own lives in saving him. But if anyone devoted himself to lifesaving in the sense of giving it his total attention—so that he thought and spoke of nothing else and demanded the cessation of all other human activities until everyone had learned to swim—he would be a monomaniac. The rescue of drowning men is, then, a duty worth dying for, but not worth living for. It seems to me that all political duties (among which I include military duties) are of this kind. A man may have to die for our country, but no man must, in any exclusive sense, live for his country. He who surrenders himself without reservation to the temporal claims of a nation, or a party, or a class is rendering to Caesar that which, of all things, most emphatically belongs to God: himself.

DYING TO SELF. Your real, new self (which is Christ's and also yours, and yours just because it is His) will not come as long as you are looking for it. It will come when you are looking for Him. Does that sound strange? The same principle holds, you know, for more everyday matters. Even in social life,

you will never make a good impression on
other people until you stop thinking about
what sort of impression you are making. Even
in literature and art, no man who bothers
about originality will ever be original:
whereas if you simply try to tell the truth
(without caring twopence how often it has
been told before) you will, nine times out of
ten, become original without ever having noticed it. The principle runs through all life
from top to bottom. Give up yourself, and
you will find your real self. Lose your life and
you will save it. Submit to death, death of
your ambitions and favourite wishes every day
and death of your whole body in the end:
submit with every fibre of your being, and
you will find eternal life. Keep back nothing.
Nothing that you have not given away will
be really yours. Nothing in you that has not
died will ever be raised from the dead. Look
for yourself, and you will find in the long
run only hatred, loneliness, despair, rage,

ruin, and decay. But look for Christ and you will find Him, and with Him everything else thrown in.

EITHER-OR. I do not think that all who choose wrong roads perish; but their rescue consists in being put back on the right road. A sum can be put right: but only by going back till you find the error and working it afresh from that point, never by simply *going on*. Evil can be undone, but it cannot 'develop' into good. Time does not heal it. The spell must be unwound, bit by bit, 'with backward mutters of dissevering power'—or else not. It is still 'either-or'. If we insist on keeping Hell (or even Earth) we shall not see Heaven: if we accept Heaven we shall not be able to retain even the smallest and most intimate souvenirs of Hell.

ENTITLEMENT. *The demon Screwtape writes:* Whatever men expect they soon come to think they have a right to: the sense of disappointment can, with very little skill on our part, be turned into a sense of injury.

EVIL. Remember that, as I said, the right direction leads not only to peace but to knowledge. When a man is getting better he understands more and more clearly the evil that is still left in him. When a man is getting worse he understands his own badness less and less. A moderately bad man knows he is not very good: a thoroughly bad man thinks he is all right. This is common sense, really. You understand sleep when you are awake, not while you are sleeping. You can see mistakes in arithmetic when your mind is working properly: while you are making them you cannot see them. You can understand the nature of drunkenness when you are sober, not when you are drunk. Good people know about both good and evil: bad people do not know about either.

FAITH. It means simply Belief—accepting or regarding as true the doctrines of Christianity. That is fairly simple. But what does puzzle people—at least it used to puzzle me—is the fact that Christians regard faith in this sense as a virtue. I used to ask how on earth it can be a virtue—what is there moral or immoral about believing or not believing a set of statements? Obviously, I used to say, a sane man accepts or rejects any statement, not because he wants to or does not want to, but because the evidence seems to him good or bad. If he were mistaken about the goodness or badness of the evidence that would not mean he was a bad man, but only that he was not very clever. And if he thought the evidence bad but tried to force himself to believe in spite of it, that would be merely stupid.

Well, I think I still take that view. But what I did not see then—and a good many people do not see still—was this. I was assuming that if the human mind once accepts a thing as true it will automatically go on regarding it as true, until some real reason for reconsidering it turns up. In fact, I was assuming that the human mind is completely ruled by reason. But that is not so. For example, my reason is perfectly convinced by good evidence that anaesthetics do not smother me and that properly trained surgeons do not start operating until I am unconscious. But that does not alter the fact that when they have me down on the table and clap their horrible mask over my face, a mere childish panic begins inside me. I start thinking I am going to choke, and I am afraid they will start cutting me up before I am properly under. In other words, I lose my faith in anaesthetics. It is not reason that is taking away my faith: on the contrary, my faith is based on reason. It is my imagination and emotions. The battle is between faith and reason on one side and emotion and imagination on the other.

FAITH OR GOOD WORKS. Christians have often disputed as to whether what leads the Christian home is good actions, or Faith in Christ. I have no right really to speak on such a difficult question, but it does seem to me like asking which blade in a pair of scissors is most necessary. A serious moral effort is the only thing that will bring you to the point where you throw up the sponge. Faith in Christ is the only thing to save you from despair at that point: and out of that Faith in Him good actions must inevitably come.

FAITH TESTED. I am not asking anyone to accept Christianity if his best reasoning tells him that the weight of the evidence is against it. That is not the point at which Faith comes in. But supposing a man's reason once decides that the weight of the evidence is for it. I can tell that man what is going to happen to him in the next few weeks. There will come a moment when there is bad news, or he is in trouble, or is living among a lot of other people who do not believe it, and all at once his emotions will rise up and carry out a sort of blitz on his belief. Or else there will come a moment when he wants a woman, or wants to tell a lie, or feels very pleased with himself, or sees a chance of making a little money in some way that is not perfectly fair: some moment, in fact, at which it would be very convenient if Christianity were not true. And once again his wishes and desires will carry out a blitz. I am not talking of moments at which any real new reasons against Christianity turn up. Those have to be faced and that is a different matter. I am talking about moments when a mere mood rises up against it.

Now Faith, in the sense in which I am here using the word, is the art of holding on to things your reason has once accepted, in spite of your changing moods. For moods will change, whatever view your reason takes.

FAITH, HOW TO KEEP. One must train the habit of Faith.

The first step is to recognise the fact that your moods change. The next is to make sure that, if you have once accepted Christianity, then some of its main doctrines shall be deliberately held before your mind for some time every day. That is why daily prayers and religious readings and churchgoing are necessary parts of the Christian life. We have to be continually reminded of what we believe. Neither this belief nor any other will automatically remain alive in the mind. It must be fed. And as a matter of fact, if you examined a hundred people who had lost their faith in Christianity, I wonder how many of them would turn out to have been reasoned out of it by honest argument? Do not most people simply drift away?

FEAR. *The demon Screwtape notes:* For remember, the *act* of cowardice is all that matters;

the emotion of fear is, in itself, no sin and, though we enjoy it, does us no good.

FORGIVENESS. It is perhaps not so hard to forgive a single great injury. But to forgive the incessant provocations of daily life—to keep on forgiving the bossy mother-in-law, the bullying husband, the nagging wife, the selfish daughter, the deceitful son—how can we do it? Only, I think, by remembering where we stand, by meaning our words when we say in our prayers each night "forgive us our trespasses as we forgive those that trespass against us." We are offered forgiveness on no other terms. To refuse it is to refuse God's mercy for ourselves. There is no hint of exceptions and God means what He says.

FORGIVENESS, REAL. Real forgiveness means looking steadily at the sin, the sin that is left over without any excuse, after all allowances have been made, and seeing it in all its horror, dirt, meanness, and malice, and nevertheless being wholly reconciled to the man who has done it. That, and only that, is forgiveness, and that we can always have from God if we ask for it.

FORGIVING VS. EXCUSING. I find that when I think I am asking God to forgive me I am often in reality (unless I watch myself very carefully) asking Him to do something quite different. I am asking Him not to forgive me but to excuse me. But there is all the difference in the world between forgiving and excusing. Forgiveness says "Yes, you have done this thing, but I accept your apology; I will never hold it against you and everything between us two will be exactly as it was before." But excusing says "I see that you couldn't help it or didn't mean it; you weren't really to blame." If one was not really to blame then there is nothing to forgive. In that sense forgiveness and excusing are almost opposites. . . .

When it comes to a question of our forgiving other people, it is partly the same and partly different. It is the same because, here also, forgiving does not mean excusing. Many people seem to think it does. They think that if you ask them to forgive someone who has cheated or bullied them you are trying to make out that that there was really no cheating or no bullying. But if that were so, there would be nothing to forgive. They keep on replying, "But I tell you the man broke a most solemn promise." Exactly: that is precisely what you have to forgive. (This doesn't mean that you must necessarily believe his next promise. It does mean that you must make every effort to kill every taste of resentment in your own heart—every wish to humiliate or hurt him or to pay him out.) The difference between this situation and the one in which you are asking God's forgiveness is this. In our own case we accept excuses too easily; in other people's we do not accept them easily enough.

FORGIVING THY NEIGHBOUR.

I said . . . that chastity was the most unpopular of the Christian virtues. But I am not sure I was right. I believe there is one even more unpopular. It is laid down in the Christian rule, 'Thou shalt love thy neighbour as thyself.' Because in Christian morals 'thy neighbour' includes 'thy enemy', and so we come up against this terrible duty of forgiving our enemies.

Every one says forgiveness is a lovely idea, until they have something to forgive, as we had during the war. And then, to mention the subject at all is to be greeted with howls of anger. It is not that people think this too high and difficult a virtue: it is that they think it hateful and contemptible. 'That sort of talk makes them sick,' they say. And half of you already want to ask me, 'I wonder how you'd feel about forgiving the Gestapo if you were a Pole or a Jew?'

So do I. I wonder very much. Just as when Christianity tells me that I must not deny my religion even to save myself from death by torture, I wonder very much what I should do when it came to the point. I am not trying to tell you . . . what I could do—I can do precious little—I am telling you what Christianity is. I did not invent it. And there, right in the middle of it, I find 'Forgive us our sins as we forgive those that sin against us.' There is no slightest suggestion that we are offered forgiveness on any other terms. It is made perfectly clear that if we do not forgive we shall not be forgiven. There are no two ways about it.

FORTITUDE. Fortitude includes both kinds of courage—the kind that faces danger as well as the kind that 'sticks it' under pain. 'Guts' is perhaps the nearest modern English. You will notice, of course, that you cannot practise any of the other virtues very long without bringing this one into play.

FREEDOM. If a thing is free to be good it is also free to be bad. And free will is what has made evil possible. Why, then, did God give them free will? Because free will, though it makes evil possible, is also the only thing that makes possible any love or goodness or joy worth having. A world of automata—of creatures that worked like machines—would hardly be worth creating. The happiness which God designs for His higher creatures is the happiness of being freely, voluntarily united to Him and to each other in an ecstasy of love and delight compared with which the most rapturous love between a man and a woman on this earth is mere milk and water. And for that they must be free.

FUTURE. Never, in peace or war, commit your virtue or your happiness to the future. Happy work is best done by the man who takes his long-term plans somewhat lightly and works from moment to moment "as to the Lord." It is only our *daily* bread that we are encouraged to ask for. The present is the only time in which any duty can be done or any grace received.

GOOD. We are not living in a world where
all roads are radii of a circle and where all, if
followed long enough, will therefore draw
gradually nearer and finally meet at the centre: rather in a world where every road, after
a few miles, forks into two, and each of those
into two again, and at each fork you must
make a decision. Even on the biological level
life is not like a river but like a tree. It does
not move towards unity but away from it and
the creatures grow further apart as they increase in perfection. Good, as it ripens, becomes continually more different not only
from evil but from other good.

GOOD AND EVIL. Good and evil both
increase at compound interest. That is why the
little decisions you and I make every day are of
such infinite importance. The smallest good
act today is the capture of a strategic point
from which, a few months later, you may be
able to go on to victories you never dreamed
of. An apparently trivial indulgence in lust or

anger today is the loss of a ridge or railway
line or bridgehead from which the enemy may
launch an attack otherwise impossible.

GOOD AND EVIL, GOD'S PURPOSE.

A merciful man aims at his neighbour's
good and so does 'God's will', consciously
co-operating with 'the simple good'. A cruel
man oppresses his neighbour, and so does
simple evil. But in doing such evil, he is used
by God, without his own knowledge or con-
sent, to produce the complex good—so that
the first man serves God as a son, and the second as a tool. For you will certainly carry out
God's purpose, however you act, but it makes
a difference to you whether you serve like
Judas or like John. The whole system is, so to
speak, calculated for the clash between good
men and bad men, and the good fruits of fortitude, patience, pity and forgiveness for
which the cruel man is permitted to be cruel,
presuppose that the good man ordinarily con-
tinues to seek simple good.

GOODNESS. God is not merely good, but goodness; goodness is not merely divine, but God.

GUILT. Christianity tells people to repent and promises them forgiveness. It therefore has nothing (as far as I know) to say to people who do not know they have done anything to repent of and who do not feel that they need any forgiveness.

HATE. *The demon Screwtape writes:* Hatred we can manage. The tension of human nerves during noise, danger, and fatigue, makes them prone to any violent emotion and it is only a question of guiding this susceptibility into the right channels. If conscience resists, muddle him. Let him say that he feels hatred not on his own behalf but on that of the women and children, and that a Christian is told to forgive his own, not other people's enemies. In other words let him consider himself sufficiently identified with the women and children to feel hatred on their behalf, but *not* sufficiently identified to regard their enemies as his own and therefore proper objects of forgiveness.

But hatred is best combined with Fear. Cowardice, alone of all the vices, is purely painful—horrible to anticipate, horrible to feel, horrible to remember; Hatred has its pleasures. It is therefore often the *compensation* by which a frightened man reimburses himself for the miseries of Fear. The more he fears, the more he will hate. And Hatred is also a great anodyne for shame. To make a deep wound in his charity, you should therefore first defeat his courage.

HEAVEN. There is no need to be worried by facetious people who try to make the Christian hope of 'Heaven' ridiculous by saying they do not want 'to spend eternity playing harps'. The answer to such people is that if they cannot understand books written for grown-ups, they should not talk about them. All the scriptural imagery (harps, crowns, gold, etc.) is, of course, a merely symbolical attempt to express the inexpressible. Musical instruments are mentioned because for many people (not all) music is the thing known in the present life which most strongly suggests ecstasy and infinity. Crowns are mentioned to suggest the fact that those who are united with God in eternity share His splendour and power and joy. Gold is mentioned to suggest the timelessness of Heaven (gold does not rust) and the preciousness of it. People who take these symbols literally might as well think that when Christ told us to be like doves, He meant that we were to lay eggs.

HEAVEN AND HELL. God will look to every soul like its first love because He is its first love. Your place in heaven will seem to be made for you and you alone, because you were made for it—made for it stitch by stitch as a glove is made for a hand.

It is from this point of view that we can understand hell in its aspect of privation. All your life an unattainable ecstasy has hovered just beyond the grasp of your consciousness. The day is coming when you will wake to find, beyond all hope, that you have attained it, or else, that it was within your reach and you have lost it forever.

HELL. In the long run the answer to all those who object to the doctrine of hell, is itself a question: 'What are you asking God to do?' To wipe out their past sins and, at all costs, to give them a fresh start, smoothing every difficulty and offering every miraculous help? But He has done so, on Calvary. To forgive them? They will not be forgiven. To leave them alone? Alas, I am afraid that is what He does.

HELL, CHOOSING. There are only two kinds of people in the end: those who say to God, "Thy will be done," and those to whom

God says, in the end, "*Thy* will be done." All that are in Hell, choose it. Without that self-choice there could be no Hell. No soul that seriously and constantly desires joy will ever miss it. Those who seek find. To those who knock it is opened.

HELL AND DAMNATION. In all discussions of Hell we keep steadily before our eyes the possible damnation, not of our enemies nor our friends (since both these disturb the reason) but of ourselves. This . . . is not about your wife or son, nor about Nero or Judas Iscariot; it is about you and me.

HOPE. Hope is one of the Theological virtues. This means that a continual looking forward to the eternal world is not (as some modern people think) a form of escapism or wishful thinking, but one of the things a Christian is meant to do. It does not mean that we are to leave the present world as it is. If you read history you will find that the

Christians who did most for the present
world were just those who thought most of
the next. The Apostles themselves, who set
on foot the conversion of the Roman Em-
pire, the great men who built up the Middle
Ages, the English Evangelicals who abolished
the Slave Trade, all left their mark on Earth,
precisely because their minds were occupied
with Heaven. It is since Christians have
largely ceased to think of the other world
that they have become so ineffective in this.
Aim at Heaven and you will get earth 'thrown
in': aim at earth and you will get neither. It
seems a strange rule, but something like it can
be seen at work in other matters. Health is
a great blessing, but the moment you make
health one of your main, direct objects you
start becoming a crank and imagining there
is something wrong with you. You are only
likely to get health provided you want other
things more—food, games, work, fun, open
air. In the same way, we shall never save
civilisation as long as civilisation is our main

object. We must learn to want something else even more.

HUMAN WILL. *The demon Screwtape writes:* Think of your man as a series of concentric circles, his will being the innermost, his intellect coming next, and finally his fantasy. You can hardly hope, at once, to exclude from all the circles everything that smells of the Enemy: but you must keep on shoving all the virtues outward till they are finally located in the circle of fantasy, and all the desirable qualities inward into the Will. It is only in so far as they reach the Will and are there embodied in habits that the virtues are really fatal to us.

HUMANITY, REDEEMED. God is not merely mending, not simply restoring a *status quo*. Redeemed humanity is to be something more glorious than unfallen humanity would have been, more glorious than any unfallen race now is (if at this moment the night sky conceals any such). The greater the sin, the greater the mercy: the deeper the death the brighter the rebirth. And this super-added glory will, with true vicariousness, exalt all creatures and those who have never fallen will thus bless Adam's fall.

HUMILITY. We must not think Pride is something God forbids because He is offended at it, or that Humility is something He demands as due to His own dignity—as if God Himself was proud. He is not in the least worried about His dignity. The point is, He wants you to know Him: wants to give you Himself. And He and you are two things of such a kind that if you really get into any kind of touch with Him you will, in fact, be humble—delightedly humble, feeling the infinite relief of having for once got rid of all the silly nonsense about your own dignity which has made you restless and unhappy all your life. He is trying to make you humble in order to make this moment possible: trying to take off a lot of silly, ugly, fancy-dress in which we have all got ourselves up and are strutting about like the little idiots we are. I wish I had got a bit further with humility myself: if I had, I could probably tell you more about the relief, the comfort, of taking the fancy-dress off—getting rid of the false self, with all its 'Look at me' and 'Aren't I a good boy?' and all its posing and posturing. To get even near it, even for a moment, is like a drink of cold water to a man in a desert.

HUMILITY, TRUE. Do not imagine that if you meet a really humble man he will be what most people call 'humble' nowadays: he will not be a sort of greasy, smarmy person, who is always telling you that, of course, he is nobody. Probably all you will think about him is that he seemed a cheerful, intelligent chap who took a real interest in what *you* said to *him*. If you do dislike him it will be because you feel a little envious of anyone who seems to enjoy life so easily. He will not be thinking about humility: he will not be thinking about himself at all.

IDEALS. When a man says that a certain woman, or house, or ship, or garden is 'his ideal' he does not mean (unless he is rather a fool) that everyone else ought to have the same ideal. In such matters we are entitled to have different tastes and, therefore, different ideals. But it is dangerous to describe a man who tries very hard to keep the moral law as a 'man of high ideals', because this might lead you to think that moral perfection was a private taste of his own and that the rest of us were not called on to share it. This would be a disastrous mistake. Perfect behaviour may be as unattainable as perfect gear-changing when we drive; but it is a necessary ideal prescribed for all men by the very nature of the human machine just as perfect gear-changing is an ideal prescribed for all drivers by the very nature of cars. And it would be even more dangerous to think of oneself as a person 'of high ideals' because one is trying to tell no lies at all (instead of only a few lies) or never to commit adultery (instead of committing it only seldom) or not to be a bully (instead of being only a moderate bully). It might lead you to become a prig and to think you were rather a special person who deserved to be congratulated on his 'idealism'.

IDOLATRY.   To love and admire anything outside yourself is to take one step away from utter spiritual ruin; though we shall not be well so long as we love and admire anything more than we love and admire God.

IMMORTALITY.   Christianity asserts that every individual human being is going to live for ever, and this must be either true or false. Now there are a good many things which would not be worth bothering about if I were going to live only seventy years, but which I had better bother about very seriously if I am going to live for ever. Perhaps my bad temper or my jealousy are gradually getting worse—so gradually that the increase in seventy years will not be very noticeable. But it might be absolute hell in a million years: in fact, if Christianity is true, Hell is the precisely correct technical term for what it would be.

IMPULSES. It is a mistake to think that some of our impulses—say mother love or patriotism—are good, and others, like sex or the fighting instinct, are bad. All we mean is that the occasions on which the fighting instinct or the sexual desire need to be restrained are rather more frequent than those for restraining mother love or patriotism. But there are situations in which it is the duty of a married man to encourage his sexual impulse and of a soldier to encourage the fighting instinct. There are also occasions on which a mother's love for her own children or a man's love for his own country have to be suppressed or they will lead to unfairness towards other people's children or countries. Strictly speaking, there are no such things as good and bad impulses. Think once again of a piano. It has not got two kinds of notes on it, the 'right' notes and the 'wrong' ones. Every single note is right at one time and wrong at another. . . .

By the way, the point is of great practical consequence. The most dangerous thing you can do is to take any one impulse of your own nature and set it up as the thing you ought to follow at all costs. There is not one of them which will not make us into devils if we set it up as an absolute guide. You might think love of humanity in general was safe, but it is not. If you leave out justice you will find yourself breaking agreements and faking evidence in trials 'for the sake of humanity', and become in the end a cruel and treacherous man.

INTERRUPTIONS. The great thing, if one can, is to stop regarding all the unpleasant things as interruptions of one's 'own', or 'real' life. The truth is of course that what one calls the interruptions are precisely one's real life— the life God is sending one day by day: what one calls one's 'real life' is a phantom of one's own imagination.

JOY. All Joy reminds. It is never a possession, always a desire for something longer ago or further away or still "about to be."

JUDGE NOT. Some of us who seem quite nice people may, in fact, have made so little use of a good heredity and a good upbringing that we are really worse than those whom we regard as fiends. Can we be quite certain how we should have behaved if we had been saddled with the psychological outfit, and then with the bad upbringing, and then with the power, say, of Himmler? That is why Christians are told not to judge. We see only the results which a man's choices make out of his raw material. But God does not judge him on the raw material at all, but on what he has done with it. Most of the man's psychological makeup is probably due to his body: when his body dies all that will fall off him, and the real central man, the thing that chose, that made the best or the worst out of this material, will stand naked. All sorts of nice things which we thought our own, but which were really due to a good digestion, will fall off some of us: all sorts of nasty things which were due to complexes or bad health will fall off others. We shall then, for the first time, see every one as he really was. There will be surprises.

JUSTICE. Justice means much more than the sort of thing that goes on in law courts. It is the old name for everything we should now call 'fairness'; it includes honesty, give and take, truthfulness, keeping promises, and all that side of life.

KINDNESS. There is kindness in Love: but Love and kindness are not coterminous, and when kindness (in the sense given above) is separated from the other elements of Love, it involves a certain fundamental indifference to its object, and even something like contempt of it. Kindness consents very readily to the removal of its object—we have all met people whose kindness to animals is constantly leading them to kill animals lest they should suffer. Kindness, merely as such, cares not whether its object becomes good or bad, provided only that it escapes suffering. As Scripture points out, it is bastards who are spoiled: the legitimate sons, who are to carry on the family tradition, are punished [Hebrews 12:8]. It is for people whom we care nothing about that we demand happiness on any terms: with our friends, our lovers, our children, we are exacting and would rather see them suffer much than be happy in contemptible and estranging modes. If God is

Love, He is, by definition, something more than mere kindness. And it appears, from all the records, that though He has often rebuked us and condemned us, He has never regarded us with contempt. He has paid us the intolerable compliment of loving us, in the deepest, most tragic, most inexorable sense.

LOVE. To love at all is to be vulnerable. Love anything, and your heart will certainly be wrung and possibly be broken. If you want to make sure of keeping it intact, you must give your heart to no one, not even to an animal. Wrap it carefully round with hobbies and little luxuries; avoid all entanglements; lock it up safe in the casket or coffin of your selfishness. But in that casket—safe, dark, motionless, airless—it will change. It will not be broken; it will become unbreakable, impenetrable, irredeemable. The alternative to tragedy, or at least to the risk of tragedy, is damnation. The only place outside Heaven where you can be perfectly safe from all the dangers and perturbations of love is Hell.

LOVE YOUR ENEMY. I imagine somebody will say, 'Well, if one is allowed to condemn the enemy's acts, and punish him, and kill him, what difference is left between Christian morality and the ordinary view?' All the difference in the world. Remember, we Christians think man lives for ever. Therefore, what really matters is those little marks or twists on the central, inside part of the soul which are going to turn it, in the long run, into a heavenly or a hellish creature. We may kill if necessary, but we must not hate and enjoy hating. We may punish if necessary, but we must not enjoy it. In other words, something inside us, the feeling of resentment, the feeling that wants to get one's own back, must be simply killed. I do not mean that anyone can decide this moment that he will never feel it any more. That is not how things happen.

I mean that every time it bobs its head up, day after day, year after year, all our lives long, we must hit it on the head. It is hard work, but the attempt is not impossible. Even while we kill and punish we must try to feel about the enemy as we feel about ourselves—to wish that he were not bad, to hope that he may, in this world or another, be cured: in fact, to wish his good. That is what is meant in the Bible by loving him: wishing his good, not feeling fond of him nor saying he is nice when he is not.

LOVE YOUR NEIGHBOUR. Do not waste time bothering whether you 'love' your neighbour; act as if you did. As soon as we do this we find one of the great secrets. When you are behaving as if you loved some-one, you will presently come to love him. If you injure someone you dislike, you will find yourself disliking him more. If you do him a good turn, you will find yourself disliking him less.

LOVE, ROMANTIC. What we call
'being in love' is a glorious state, and, in several ways, good for us. It helps to make us
generous and courageous, it opens our eyes
not only to the beauty of the beloved but to
all beauty, and it subordinates (especially at
first) our merely animal sexuality; in that
sense, love is the great conqueror of lust. No
one in his senses would deny that being in
love is far better than either common sensual-
ity or cold self-centredness. But, as I said before, 'the most dangerous thing you can do is
to take any one impulse of our own nature
and set it up as the thing you ought to follow
at all costs'. Being in love is a good thing, but
it is not the best thing. There are many things
below it, but there are also things above it.
You cannot make it the basis of a whole life.
It is a noble feeling, but it is still a feeling.
Now no feeling can be relied on to last in its
full intensity, or even to last at all. Knowledge
can last, principles can last, habits can last; but
feelings come and go. And in fact, whatever

people say, the state called 'being in love' usually does not last. If the old fairy-tale ending 'They lived happily ever after' is taken to mean 'They felt for the next fifty years exactly as they felt the day before they were married', then it says what probably never was nor ever would be true, and would be highly undesirable if it were.

MARRIAGE. The Christian idea of marriage is based on Christ's words that a man and wife are to be regarded as a single organism—for that is what the words 'one flesh' would be in modern English. And the Christians believe that when He said this He was not expressing a sentiment but stating a fact—just as one is stating a fact when one says that a lock and its key are one mechanism, or that a violin and a bow are one musical instrument. The inventor of the human machine was telling us that its two halves, the male and the female, were made to be combined together in pairs, not simply on the sexual level, but totally combined. The monstrosity of sexual intercourse outside marriage is that those who indulge in it are trying to isolate one kind of union (the sexual) from all the other kinds of union which were intended to go along with it and make up the total union. The Christian attitude does not mean that there is anything wrong about sexual pleasure, any more than about the pleasure of eating. It means that you must not isolate that pleasure and try to get it by itself, any more than you ought to try to get the pleasures of taste without swallowing and, digesting, by chewing things and spitting them out again.

MODESTY. The Christian rule of chastity must not be confused with the social rule of 'modesty' (in one sense of that word); i.e. propriety, or decency. The social rule of propriety lays down how much of the human body should be displayed and what subjects can be referred to, and in what words, according to the customs of a given social circle. Thus, while the rule of chastity is the same for all Christians at all times, the rule of propriety changes. . . . When people break the rule of propriety current in their own time and place, if they do so in order to excite lust in themselves or others, then they are offending against chastity. But if they break it through ignorance or carelessness they are guilty only of bad manners. When, as often happens, they break it defiantly in order to shock or embarrass others, they are not necessarily being unchaste, but they are being uncharitable: for it is uncharitable to take pleasure in making other people uncomfortable.

MONEY. Christ said 'Blessed are the poor' and 'How hard it is for the rich to enter the Kingdom,' and no doubt He primarily meant the economically rich and economically poor. But do not His words also apply to another kind of riches and poverty? One of the dangers of having a lot of money is that you may be quite satisfied with the kinds of happiness money can give and so fail to realise your need for God. If everything seems to come simply by signing cheques, you may forget that you are at every moment totally dependent on God. Now quite plainly, natural gifts carry with them a similar danger. If you have sound nerves and intelligence and health and popularity and a good upbringing, you are likely to be quite satisfied with your character as it is. 'Why drag God into it?' you may ask. A certain level of good conduct comes fairly easily to you. You are not one of those wretched creatures who are always being tripped up by sex, or dipsomania, or nervousness, or bad temper. Everyone says you are a nice chap and (between ourselves) you agree with them. You are quite likely to believe that all this niceness is your own doing: and you may easily not feel the need for any better kind of goodness. Often people who have all these natural kinds of goodness cannot be brought to recognise their need for Christ at all until, one day, the natural goodness lets them down and their self-satisfaction is shattered. In other words, it is hard for those who are 'rich' in this sense to enter the Kingdom.

MORALITY. People often think of Christian morality as a kind of bargain in which God says, 'If you keep a lot of rules I'll reward you, and if you don't I'll do the other thing.' I do not think that is the best way of looking at it. I would much rather say that every time you make a choice you are turning the central part of you, the part of you that chooses, into something a little different from what it was before. And taking your life as a whole, with all your innumerable choices, all your life long you are slowly turning this central thing either into a heavenly creature or

into a hellish creature: either into a creature
that is in harmony with God, and with other
creatures, and with itself, or else into one that
is in a state of war and hatred with God, and
with its fellow-creatures, and with itself. To
be the one kind of creature is heaven: that is,
it is joy and peace and knowledge and power.
To be the other means madness, horror, id-
iocy, rage, impotence, and eternal loneliness.
Each of us at each moment is progressing to
the one state or the other.

NICE. If you are a nice person—if virtue
comes easily to you—beware! Much is expected from those to whom much is given. If
you mistake for your own merits what are really God's gifts to you through nature, and
if you are contented with simply being nice,
you are still a rebel: and all those gifts will
only make your fall more terrible, your cor-
ruption more complicated, your bad example
more disastrous. The Devil was an archangel

once; his natural gifts were as far above yours as yours are above those of a chimpanzee.

But if you are a poor creature—poisoned by a wretched upbringing in some house full of vulgar jealousies and senseless quarrels— saddled, by no choice of your own, with some loathsome sexual perversion—nagged day in and day out by an inferiority complex that makes you snap at your best friends—do not despair. He knows all about it. You are one of the poor whom He blessed. He knows what a wretched machine you are trying to drive. Keep on. Do what you can. One day (perhaps in another world, but perhaps far sooner than that) He will fling it on the scrap- heap and give you a new one. And then you may astonish us all—not least yourself: for you have learned your driving in a hard school. (Some of the last will be first and some of the first will be last).

OBEDIENCE. I think that many of us, when Christ has enabled us to overcome one or two sins that were an obvious nuisance, are inclined to feel (though we do not put it into words) that we are now good enough. He has done all we wanted Him to do, and we should be obliged if He would now leave us alone. As we say 'I never expected to be a saint, I only wanted to be a decent ordinary chap.' And we imagine when we say this that we are being humble.

But this is the fatal mistake. Of course we never wanted, and never asked, to be made into the sort of creatures He is going to make us into. But the question is not what we intended ourselves to be, but what He intended us to be when He made us. He is the inventor, we are only the machine. He is the painter, we are only the picture. How should we know what He means us to be like? You see, He has already made us something very different from what we were. Long ago, before we were born, when we were inside our mothers' bodies, we passed through various stages. We were once rather like vegetables, and once rather like fish: it was only at a later stage that we became like human babies. And if we had been conscious at those earlier stages, I daresay we should have been quite contented to stay as vegetables or fish—should not have wanted to be made into babies. But all the time He knew His plan for us and was determined to carry it out. Something the same is now happening at a higher level. We may be content to remain what we call 'ordinary people': but He is determined to carry out a quite different plan. To shrink back from that plan is not humility: it is laziness and cowardice. To submit to it is not conceit or megalomania; it is obedience.

PAIN. Pain is not only immediately recognisable evil, but evil impossible to ignore. We can rest contentedly in our sins and in our stupidities; and anyone who has watched gluttons shovelling down the most exquisite foods as if they did not know what they were eating, will admit that we can ignore even pleasure. But pain insists upon being attended to. God whispers to us in our pleasures, speaks in our conscience, but shouts in our pain: it is His megaphone to rouse a deaf world.

PAIN, PURPOSES OF. If the first and lowest operation of pain shatters the illusion that all is well, the second shatters the illusion that what we have, whether good or bad in itself, is our own and enough for us. Everyone has noticed how hard it is to turn our thoughts to God when everything is going well with us. We 'have all we want' is a terrible saying when 'all' does not include God. We find God an interruption. As St Augustine says somewhere, 'God wants to give us something, but cannot, because our hands are full—there's nowhere for Him to put it.' Or as a friend of mine said, 'We regard God as an airman regards his parachute; it's there for emergencies but he hopes he'll never have to use it.' Now God, who has made us, knows what we are and that our happiness lies in Him. Yet we will not seek it in Him as long as he leaves us any other resort where it can even plausibly be looked for. While what we call 'our own life' remains agreeable we will not surrender it to Him. What then can God do in our interests but make 'our own life' less agreeable to us, and take away the plausible source of false happiness?

PEER PRESSURE. I wonder whether, in ages of promiscuity, many a virginity has not been lost less in obedience to Venus than in obedience to the lure of the caucus. For, of course, when promiscuity is the fashion, the chaste are outsiders. They are ignorant of something that other people know. They are uninitiated. And as for lighter matters, the number who first smoked or first got drunk for a similar reason is probably very large.

PERFECTION. On the one hand, God's demand for perfection need not discourage you in the least in your present attempts to be good, or even in your present failures. Each time you fall He will pick you up again. And He knows perfectly well that your own efforts are never going to bring you anywhere near perfection. On the other hand, you must realise from the outset that the goal towards which He is beginning to guide you is absolute perfection; and no power in the whole universe, except you yourself, can prevent Him from taking you to that goal. That is what you are in for. And it is very important to realise that. If we do not, then we are very likely to start pulling back and resisting Him after a certain point.

PERFECTION, ATTAINMENT OF.
We may, indeed, be sure that perfect chastity—like perfect charity—will not be attained by any merely human efforts. You must ask for God's help. Even when you have done so, it may seem to you for a long time that no help,

or less help than you need, is being given.
Never mind. After each failure, ask forgiveness, pick yourself up, and try again. Very
often what God first helps us towards is not
the virtue itself but just this power of always
trying again. For however important chastity
(or courage, or truthfulness, or any other
virtue) may be, this process trains us in habits
of the soul which are more important still. It
cures our illusions about ourselves and teaches
us to depend on God. We learn, on the one
hand, that we cannot trust ourselves even in
our best moments, and, on the other, that we
need not despair even in our worst, for our
failures are forgiven. The only fatal thing is
to sit down content with anything less than
perfection.

PERSEVERANCE. If we are all going to
be destroyed by an atomic bomb, let that
bomb when it comes find us doing sensible
and human things—praying, working, teach-

ing, reading, listening to music, bathing the children, playing tennis, chatting to our friends over a pint and a game of darts—not huddled together like frightened sheep and thinking about bombs. They may break our bodies (a microbe can do that) but they need not dominate our minds.

POWER. The descent to hell is easy, and those who begin by worshipping power soon worship evil.

PRAYER. The prayer preceding all prayers is "May it be the real I who speaks. May it be the real Thou that I speak to." Infinitely various are the levels from which we pray. Emotional intensity is in itself no proof of spiritual depth. If we pray in terror we shall pray earnestly; it only proves that terror is an earnest emotion. Only God Himself can let the bucket down to the depths in us. And, on the other side, He must constantly work as the iconoclast. Every idea of Him we form, He must in mercy shatter. The most blessed result of prayer would be to rise thinking "But I never knew before. I never dreamed . . ."

PRETENDING.   What is the good of pretending to be what you are not? Well, even on the human level, you know, there are two kinds of pretending. There is a bad kind, where the pretence is there instead of the real thing; as when a man pretends he is going to help you instead of really helping you. But there is also a good kind, where the pretence leads up to the real thing. When you are not feeling particularly friendly but know you ought to be, the best thing you can do, very often, is to put on a friendly manner and behave as if you were a nicer person than you actually are. And in a few minutes, as we have all noticed, you will be really feeling friendlier than you were. Very often the only way to get a quality in reality is to start behaving as if

you had it already. That is why children's
games are so important. They are always pretending to be grown-ups—playing soldiers,
playing shop. But all the time, they are hard-
ening their muscles and sharpening their wits
so that the pretence of being grown-up helps
them to grow up in earnest.

Now, the moment you realise 'Here I am,
dressing up as Christ,' it is extremely likely
that you will see at once some way in which
at that very moment the pretence could be
made less of a pretence and more of a reality.
You will find several things going on in your
mind which would not be going on there if
you were really a son of God. Well, stop
them. Or you may realise that, instead of saying your prayers, you ought to be downstairs
writing a letter, or helping your wife to wash-
up. Well, go and do it.

You see what is happening. The Christ
Himself, the Son of God who is man (just
like you) and God (just like His Father) is

actually at your side and is already at that moment beginning to turn your pretence into a reality.

PRIDE. There is one vice of which no man in the world is free; which every one in the world loathes when he sees it in someone else; and of which hardly any people, except Christians, ever imagine that they are guilty themselves. I have heard people admit that they are bad-tempered, or that they cannot keep their heads about girls or drink, or even that they are cowards. I do not think I have ever heard anyone who was not a Christian accuse himself of this vice. And at the same time I have very seldom met anyone, who was not a Christian, who showed the slightest mercy to it in others. There is no fault which makes a man more unpopular, and no fault which we are more unconscious of in ourselves. And the more we have it ourselves, the more we dislike it in others.

The vice I am talking of is Pride or Self-Conceit: and the virtue opposite to it, in Christian morals, is called Humility. You may remember, when I was talking about sexual morality, I warned you that the centre of Christian morals did not lie there. Well, now, we have come to the centre. According to Christian teachers, the essential vice, the utmost evil, is Pride. Unchastity, anger, greed, drunkenness, and all that, are mere fleabites in comparison: it was through Pride that the devil became the devil: Pride leads to every other vice: it is the complete anti-God state of mind.

PRIDE, ESSENCE OF. If you want to find out how proud you are the easiest way is to ask yourself, 'How much do I dislike it when other people snub me, or refuse to take any notice of me, or shove their oar in, or patronise me, or show off?' The point is that each person's pride is in competition with every one else's pride. It is because I wanted to be the big noise at the party that I am so annoyed at someone else being the big noise. Two of a trade never agree. Now what you want to get clear is that Pride is *essentially* competitive—is competitive by its very nature—while the other vices are competitive only, so to speak, by accident. Pride gets no pleasure out of having something, only out of having more of it than the next man. We say that people are proud of being rich, or clever, or good-looking, but they are not. They are proud of being richer, or cleverer, or better-looking than others. If everyone else became equally rich, or clever, or good-looking there would be nothing to be proud about. It is the comparison that makes you proud: the pleasure of being above the rest. Once the element of competition has gone, pride has gone. That is why I say that Pride is essentially competitive in a way the other vices are not. The sexual impulse may drive two men into

competition if they both want the same girl.
But that is only by accident; they might
just as likely have wanted two different girls.
But a proud man will take your girl from
you, not because he wants her, but just to
prove to himself that he is a better man than
you. Greed may drive men into competition
if there is not enough to go round; but the
proud man, even when he has got more than
he can possibly want, will try to get still more
just to assert his power. Nearly all those evils
in the world which people put down to
greed or selfishness are really far more the
result of Pride.

PRIDE, FALSE. A man is never so proud
as when striking an attitude of humility.

PROGRESS. We all want progress. But
progress means getting nearer to the place
where you want to be. And if you have taken
a wrong turning, then to go forward does not

get you any nearer. If you are on the wrong road, progress means doing an about-turn and walking back to the right road; and in that case the man who turns back soonest is the most progressive man. We have all seen this when doing arithmetic. When I have started a sum the wrong way, the sooner I admit this and go back and start again, the faster I shall get on. There is nothing progressive about being pig headed and refusing to admit a mistake. And I think if you look at the present state of the world, it is pretty plain that humanity has been making some big mistake. We are on the wrong road. And if that is so, we must go back. Going back is the quickest way on.

PRUDENCE. Prudence means practical common sense, taking the trouble to think out what you are doing and what is likely to come of it. Nowadays most people hardly think of Prudence as one of the 'virtues'. In fact, because Christ said we could only get into His world by being like children, many Christians have the idea that, provided you are 'good', it does not matter being a fool. But that is a misunderstanding. In the first place, most children show plenty of 'prudence' about doing the things they are really interested in, and think them out quite sensibly. In the second place, as St Paul points out, Christ never meant that we were to remain children in *intelligence:* on the contrary. He told us to be not only 'as harmless as doves', but also 'as wise as serpents'. He wants a child's heart, but a grown-up's head. He wants us to be simple, single-minded, affectionate, and teachable, as good children are; but He also wants every bit of intelligence we have to be alert at its job, and in first-class fighting trim. The fact that you are giving money to a charity does not mean that you need not try to find out whether that charity is a fraud or not. The fact that what you are thinking about is God Himself (for example, when you are praying) does not mean that you can be content with the same babyish ideas which you had when you were a five-year-old. It is, of course, quite true that God will not love you any the less, or have less use for you, if you happen to have been born with a very second-rate brain. He has room for people with very little sense, but He wants every one to use what sense they have.

REPENTANCE. What was the sort of 'hole' man had got himself into? He had tried to set up on his own, to behave as if he belonged to himself. In other words, fallen man is not simply an imperfect creature who needs improvement: he is a rebel who must lay down his arms. Laying down your arms, surrendering, saying you are sorry, realising that you have been on the wrong track and getting ready to start life over again from the ground floor—that is the only way out of our 'hole'.

This process of surrender—this movement full speed astern—is what Christians call repentance. Now repentance is no fun at all. It is something much harder than merely eating humble pie. It means unlearning all the self-conceit and self-will that we have been training ourselves into for thousands of years. It means killing part of yourself, undergoing a kind of death. In fact, it needs a good man to repent. And here comes the catch. Only a bad person needs to repent: only a good person can repent perfectly. The worse you are the more you need it and the less you can do it. The only person who could do it perfectly would be a perfect person—and he would not need it.

SADNESS. My own idea, for what it is worth, is that all sadness which is not either arising from the repentance of a concrete sin and hastening towards concrete amendment or restitution, or else arising from pity and

hastening to active assistance, is simply bad;
and I think we all sin by needlessly disobeying
the apostolic injunction to 'rejoice' as much
as by anything else.

SECURITY. The settled happiness and
security which we all desire, God withholds
from us by the very nature of the world:
but joy, pleasure, and merriment, He has scat-
tered broadcast. We are never safe, but we
have plenty of fun, and some ecstasy. It is
not hard to see why. The security we crave
would teach us to rest our hearts in this world
and oppose an obstacle to our return to God:
a few moments of happy love, a landscape, a
symphony, a merry meeting with our friends,
a bathe or a football match, have no such
tendency. Our Father refreshes us on the
journey with some pleasant inns, but will not
encourage us to mistake them for home.

SELF-DENIAL. We are told to deny ourselves and to take up our crosses in order that

we may follow Christ; and nearly every description of what we shall ultimately find if we do so contains an appeal to desire. If there lurks in most modern minds the notion that to desire our own good and earnestly to hope for the enjoyment of it is a bad thing, I submit that this notion . . . is no part of the Christian faith. Indeed, if we consider the unblushing promises of reward and the staggering nature of the rewards promised in the Gospels, it would seem that Our Lord finds our desires not too strong, but too weak. We are half-hearted creatures, fooling about with drink and sex and ambition when infinite joy is offered us, like an ignorant child who wants to go on making mud pies in a slum because he cannot imagine what is meant by the offer of a holiday at the sea. We are far too easily pleased.

SELF-SUFFICIENCY. The dangers of apparent self-sufficiency explain why Our Lord regards the vices of the feckless and dissipated so much more leniently than the vices that lead to worldly success. Prostitutes are in no danger of finding their present life so satisfactory that they cannot turn to God: the proud, the avaricious, the self-righteous, are in that danger.

SEX. They tell you sex has become a mess because it was hushed up. But for the last twenty years it has not been. It has been chattered about all day long. Yet it is still in a mess. If hushing up had been the cause of the trouble, ventilation would have set it right. But it has not. I think it is the other way round. I think the human race originally hushed it up because it had become such a mess. Modern people are always saying, 'Sex is nothing to be ashamed of.' They may mean two things. They may mean 'There is nothing to be ashamed of in the fact that the human race reproduces itself in a certain way, nor in the fact that it gives pleasure.' If they mean that, they are right. Christianity says the same. It is not the thing, nor the pleasure, that is the trouble. The old Christian teachers said that if man had never fallen, sexual pleasure, instead of being less than it is now, would actually have been greater. I know some muddle-headed Christians have talked as if Christianity thought that sex, or the body, or pleasure, were bad in themselves. But they were wrong. Christianity is almost the only one of the great religions which thoroughly approves of the body—which believes that matter is good, that God Himself once took on a human body, that some kind of body is going to be given to us even in Heaven and is going to be an essential part of our happiness, or beauty and our energy. Christianity has glorified marriage more than any other religion: and nearly all the greatest love poetry in the world has been produced by Christians. If anyone says that sex, in itself, is bad, Christianity contradicts him at once.

SHAME. I sometimes think that shame, mere awkward, senseless shame, does as much towards preventing good acts and straightforward happiness as any our vices can do.

SIN. We have a strange illusion that mere time cancels sin. I have heard others, and I have heard myself, recounting cruelties and falsehoods committed in boyhood as if they were no concern of the present speaker's, and even with laughter. But mere time does nothing either to the fact or to the guilt of a sin. The guilt is washed out not by time but by repentance and the blood of Christ: if we have repented these early sins we should remember the price of our forgiveness and be humble. As for the fact of a sin, is it probable that anything cancels it? All times are eternally present to God. Is it not at least possible that along some one line of His multi-dimensional eternity He sees you forever in the nursery pulling the wings off a fly, forever toadying,

lying, and lusting as a schoolboy, forever in
that moment of cowardice or insolence as a
subaltern? It may be that salvation consists not
in the cancelling of these eternal moments
but in the perfected humanity that bears the
shame forever, rejoicing in the occasion
which it furnished to God's compassion and
glad that it should be common knowledge to
the universe. Perhaps in that eternal moment
St Peter—he will forgive me if I am wrong—
forever denies his Master. If so, it would indeed be true that the joys of Heaven are for
most of us, in our present condition, 'an ac-
quired taste'—and certain ways of life may
render the taste impossible of acquisition.
Perhaps the lost are those who dare not go to
such a *public* place. Of course I do not know
that this is true; but I think the possibility is
worth keeping in mind.

SIN, AWARENESS OF. A recovery of
the old sense of sin is essential to Christianity.

Christ takes it for granted that men are bad.
Until we really feel this assumption of His to
be true, though we are part of the world He
came to save, we are not part of the audience
to whom His words are addressed. We lack
the first condition for understanding what
He is talking about. And when men attempt
to be Christians without this preliminary consciousness of sin, the result is almost bound to
be a certain resentment against God as to one
always inexplicably angry. Most of us have at
times felt a secret sympathy with the dying
farmer who replied to the Vicar's dissertation
on repentance by asking 'What harm have I
ever done *Him?'* There is the real rub. The
worst we have done to God is to leave Him
alone—why can't He return the compliment?
Why not live and let live? What call has He,
of all beings, to be 'angry'? It's easy for Him
to be good!

SIN, BASIC. From the moment a creature
becomes aware of God as God and of itself as

self, the terrible alternative of choosing God
or self for the centre is opened to it. This sin
is committed daily by young children and
ignorant peasants as well as by sophisticated
persons, by solitaries no less than by those who
live in society: it is the fall in every individual
life, and in each day of each individual life, the
basic sin behind all particular sins: at this very
moment you and I are either committing it,
or about to commit it, or repenting it.

SIN, WORK OF.   That explains what
always used to puzzle me about Christian
writers; they seem to be so very strict at one
moment and so very free and easy at another.
They talk about mere sins of thought as if
they were immensely important: and then
they talk about the most frightful murders and
treacheries as if you had only got to repent
and all would be forgiven. But I have come to
see that they are right. What they are always
thinking of is the mark which the action
leaves on that tiny central self which no one

sees in this life but which each of us will have to endure—or enjoy—for ever. One man may be so placed that his anger sheds the blood of thousands, and another so placed that however angry he gets he will only be laughed at. But the little mark on the soul may be much the same in both. Each has done something to himself which, unless he repents, will make it harder for him to keep out of the rage next time he is tempted, and will make the rage worse when he does fall into it. Each of them, if he seriously turns to God, can have that twist in the central man straightened out again: each is, in the long run, doomed if he will not. The bigness or smallness of the thing, seen from the outside, is not what really matters.

SIN AND SINNER. I remember Christian teachers telling me long ago that I must hate a bad man's actions, but not hate the bad man: or, as they would say, hate the sin but not the sinner.

For a long time I used to think this a silly, straw-splitting distinction: how could you hate what a man did and not hate the man? But years later it occurred to me that there was one man to whom I had been doing this all my life—namely myself. However much I might dislike my own cowardice or conceit or greed, I went on loving myself. There had never been the slightest difficulty about it. In fact the very reason why I hated the things was that I loved the man. Just because I loved myself, I was sorry to find that I was the sort of man who did those things. Consequently, Christianity does not want us to reduce by one atom the hatred we feel for cruelty and treachery. We ought to hate them. Not one word of what we have said about them needs to be unsaid. But it does want us to hate them in the same way in which we hate things in ourselves: being sorry that the man should have done such things, and hoping, if it is anyway possible, that somehow, sometime, somewhere he can be cured and made human again.

SINFULNESS. We begin to notice, besides our particular sinful acts, our sinfulness; begin to be alarmed not only about what we do, but about what we are. This may sound rather difficult, so I will try to make it clear from my own case. When I come to my evening prayers and try to reckon up the sins of the day, nine times out of ten the most obvious one is some sin against charity; I have sulked or snapped or sneered or snubbed or stormed. And the excuse that immediately springs to my mind is that the provocation was so sudden and unexpected; I was caught off my guard, I had not time to collect myself. Now that may be an extenuating circumstance as regards those particular acts: they would obviously be worse if they had been deliberate and premeditated. On the other hand, surely what a man does when he is taken off his guard is the best evidence for what sort of a man he is? Surely what pops out before the man has time to put on a disguise is the truth? If there are rats in a cellar you are most likely to see them if you go in very suddenly. But the suddenness does not create the rats: it only prevents them from hiding. In the same way the suddenness of the provocation does not make me an ill-tempered man; it only shows me what an ill-tempered man I am. The rats are always there in the cellar, but if you go in shouting and noisily they will have taken cover before you switch on the light. Apparently the rats of resentment and vindictiveness are always there in the cellar of my soul. Now that cellar is out of reach of my conscious will. I can to some extent control my acts: I have no direct control over my temperament. And if (as I said before) what we are matters even more than what we do—if, indeed, what we do matters chiefly as evidence of what we are—then it follows that the change which I most need to undergo is a change that my own direct, voluntary efforts cannot bring about. And this applies to my good actions too. How many of them were done for the right motive? How many for fear of public opinion, or a desire to show off? How many from a sort of obstinacy or sense of superiority which, in different circumstances, might equally have led to some very bad act? But I cannot, by direct moral effort, give myself new motives. After the first few steps in the Christian life we realise that everything which really needs to be done in our souls can be done only by God.

TEMPERANCE. Temperance is, unfortunately, one of those words that has changed its meaning. It now usually means teetotalism. But in the days when the second Cardinal virtue was christened 'Temperance', it meant nothing of the sort. Temperance referred not specially to drink, but to all pleasures; and it meant not abstaining, but going the right length and no further. It is a mistake to think that Christians ought all to be teetotallers; Mohammedanism, not Christianity, is the teetotal religion. Of course it may be the duty of a particular Christian, or of any Christian, at a particular time, to abstain from strong drink, either because he is the sort of man who cannot drink at all without drinking too much, or because he is with people who are inclined to drunkenness and must not encourage them by drinking himself. But the whole point is that he is abstaining, for a good reason, from something which he does not condemn and which he likes to see other people enjoying. One of the marks of a certain type of bad man is that he cannot give up a thing himself without wanting every one else to give it up. That is not the Christian way. An individual Christian may see fit to give up all sorts of things for special reasons— marriage, or meat, or beer, or the cinema; but the moment he starts saying the things are bad in themselves, or looking down his nose at other people who do use them, he has taken the wrong turning.

One great piece of mischief has been done by the modern restriction of the word Temperance to the question of drink. It helps people to forget that you can be just as intemperate about lots of other things. A man who makes his golf or his motor-bicycle the centre of his life, or a woman who devotes all her thoughts to clothes or bridge or her dog, is being just as 'intemperate' as someone who gets drunk every evening. Of course, it does not show on the outside so easily: bridge-mania or golf-mania do not make you fall down in the middle of the road. But God is not deceived by externals.

TEMPTATION.   You may remember I said that the first step towards humility was to realise that one is proud. I want to add now that the next step is to make some serious attempt to practise the Christian virtues. A week is not enough. Things often go swimmingly for the first week. Try six weeks. By that time, having, as far as one can see, fallen back completely or even fallen lower than the point one began from, one will have discovered some truths about oneself. No man knows how bad he is till he has tried very hard to be good. A silly idea is current that good people do not know what temptation means. This is an obvious lie. Only those who try to resist temptation know how strong it is. After all, you find out the strength of the German army by fighting against it, not by giving in. You find out the strength of a wind by trying to talk against it, not by lying down. A man who gives in to temptation after five minutes simply does not know what it would have been like an hour later. That is why bad people, in one sense, know very little about badness. They have lived a sheltered life by always giving in. We never find out the strength of the evil impulse inside us until we try to fight it: and Christ, because He was the only man who never yielded to temptation, is also the only man who knows to the full what temptation means—the only complete realist.

TEMPTATION, OVERCOMING. I know all about the despair of overcoming chronic temptations. It is not serious provided self-offended petulance, annoyance at breaking records, impatience etc. doesn't get the upper hand. *No amount* of falls will really undo us if we keep picking ourselves up each time. We shall of course be v. muddy and tattered children by the time we reach home. But the bathrooms are all ready, the towels put out, & the clean clothes are in the airing cupboard. The only fatal thing is to lose one's temper and give it up. It is when we notice the dirt that God is most present to us: it is the v. sign of His presence.

TRANSFORMATION. Imagine yourself as a living house. God comes in to rebuild that house. At first, perhaps, you can understand what He is doing. He is getting the drains right and stopping the leaks in the roof and so on: you knew that those jobs needed doing and so you are not surprised. But presently he starts knocking the house about in a way that hurts abominably and does not seem to make sense. What on earth is He up to? The explanation is that He is building quite a different house from the one you thought of—throwing out a new wing here, putting on an extra floor there, running up towers, making courtyards. You thought you were going to be made into a decent little cottage: but He is building a palace. He intends to come and live in it Himself.

The command *Be ye perfect* is not idealistic gas. Nor is it a command to do the impossible. He is going to make us into creatures that can obey that command. He said (in the Bible) that we were 'gods' and He is going to make good His words. If we let Him—for we can prevent Him, if we choose—He will make the feeblest and filthiest of us into a god or goddess, a dazzling, radiant, immortal creature, pulsating all through with such energy and joy and wisdom and love as we cannot now imagine, a bright stainless mirror which reflects back to God perfectly (though, of course, on a smaller scale) His

C. S. LEWIS

own boundless power and delight and goodness. The process will be long and in parts
very painful, but that is what we are in for.
Nothing less. He meant what He said.

TRIBULATION. My own experience is
something like this. I am progressing along
the path of life in my ordinary contentedly
fallen and godless condition, absorbed in a
merry meeting with my friends for the mor-
row or a bit of work that tickles my vanity
today, a holiday or a new book, when suddenly a stab of abdominal pain that threatens
serious disease, or a headline in the newspa-
pers that threatens us all with destruction,
sends this whole pack of cards tumbling
down. At first I am overwhelmed, and all my
little happinesses look like broken toys. Then,
slowly and reluctantly, bit by bit, I try to bring
myself into the frame of mind that I should
be in at all times. I remind myself that all
these toys were never intended to possess my

90

heart, that my true good is in another world and my only real treasure is Christ. And perhaps, by God's grace, I succeed, and for a day or two become a creature consciously dependent on God and drawing its strength from the right sources. But the moment the threat is withdrawn, my whole nature leaps back to the toys: I am even anxious, God forgive me, to banish from my mind the only thing that supported me under the threat because it is now associated with the misery of those few days. Thus the terrible necessity of tribulation is only too clear. God has had me for but forty-eight hours and then only by dint of taking everything else away from me. Let Him but sheathe that sword for a moment and I behave like a puppy when the hated bath is over—I shake myself as dry as I can and race off to reacquire my comfortable dirtiness, if not in the nearest manure heap, at least in the nearest flower bed. And that is why tribulations cannot cease until God either sees us remade or sees that our remaking is now hopeless.

VIRTUE. Virtue—even attempted virtue—brings light; indulgence brings fog.

VIRTUES. If . . . you are ever tempted to think that we modern Western Europeans cannot really be so very bad because we are, comparatively speaking, humane—if, in other words, you think God might be content with us on that ground—ask yourself whether you think God ought to have been content with the cruelty of cruel ages because they excelled in courage or chastity. You will see at once that this is an impossibility. From considering how the cruelty of our ancestors looks to us, you may get some inkling how our softness, worldliness, and timidity would have looked to them, and hence how both must look to God.

Clive Staples Lewis (1898–1963) was one of the intellectual giants of the twentieth century and arguably the most influential Christian writer of his day. He was a Fellow and Tutor in English literature at Oxford University until 1954, when he was unanimously elected to the Chair of Medieval and Renaissance English at Cambridge University, a position he held until his retirement. He wrote more than thirty books, allowing him to reach a vast audience, and his works continue to attract thousands of new readers every year. His most distinguished and popular accomplishments include *The Chronicle of Narnia, Out of the Silent Planet, The Four Loves, The Screwtape Letters,* and *Mere Christianity.* www.cslewis.com

INDEX OF

SOURCES QUOTED

MAKE SURE TO READ THESE TIMELESS TITLES FROM C. S. LEWIS

To receive notice of events and
new books by C. S. Lewis, sign up
for C. S. Lewis's AuthorTracker
at www.authortracker.com.

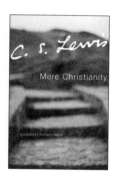

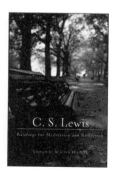